Living in a High Vibration

(Change your Vibration, Change your Life)

By S. D. Raine

Introduction

Our purpose on this planet is to forever remain a student, because your potential as the Universe is infinite. This is not to fear or be frustrated about, this is the exciting part of life that it is forever a journey, and the destination is never final.

Living what you truly enjoy and living in your truth is hardly an easy path in the way that people seek luxury, but it is immensely rewarding. It leaves a sparkle in the eye at the end of a long day, and really, we're all ultimately here to light up the world.

To be enlightened is to be at peace with the is, and to find the beauty in every moment, person, experience, and lesson, because no matter how dark life may get, if your light is always shining you will always find your way. Just be appreciative of the adversity, and grateful for the beauty, and you will be just fine

Synopsis

Your energy and vibration is something you put out into the world. It either uplifts or drains others. When you notice this interconnection, how we affect one another, we start to take more responsibility for the energy we radiate. Surround yourself only with those who encourage and sustain you, unless you are asking for the challenge to grow in your field of vibrational awareness. This will help you value yourself and raise your vibration to that of unconditional love.

We all have access to the life-force energy that will assist us in our own healing. We can also act as a channel for transmitting this energy to others. Be courageous enough to grow into the person you are meant to be. Long is the journey, and it is always safer not to go on that journey because unknown is the path, nothing is guaranteed.

Don't put limits on what wonderful things the Universe can bestow. Cast your net wide and see what fantastic opportunities you might catch. Invite the energies of expansion, manifestation, and abundance and take comfort in knowing that you are cherished.

Albert Einstein has said that "Everything in Life is Vibration." Also, we need to learn how to trust our vibration because energy doesn't lie. Lastly, learning a new lesson sets a huge amount of energy free.

Table of Contents

Chapter 1 – What is Energy, Vibration, and Frequency   1

Chapter 2 – The Differences between Vibration and Energy 19

Chapter 3 – The Three types of Energy in the Universe   33

Chapter 4 – Understanding and Transmitting Energy   42

Chapter 5 – The Benefits of Being in a High Vibration   67

Chapter 6 – Effective Ways to Raise your Vibration   77

Chapter 7 – Vibrational Medicine   87

Chapter 8 – What I have Learned   94

Summary   123

Acknowledgements

Writing a book is harder than I thought but at the same time immensely rewarding. None of this would have been possible without the support and encouragement of the people in my life that I can call my true friends.

I am forever grateful to Margaret who spent hours upon hours going through my book to ensure it was print and reader ready. She has been an integral part to my book coming to fruition.

Special thanks to Dr. Noah Beaudry and Margaret Kadej who have given me honest feedback pertaining to my book as I bit my lip. They have been with me every step of the way on my journey towards making " Living in a High Vibration", become a reality.

Chapter 1

What is Energy, Vibration, and Frequency

The Universal Law states that everything in the Universe moves and vibrates – everything is vibrating at one speed or another. Nothing rests, and everything you see around you is vibrating at one frequency or another and so are you.

The Universe is energy. Out of energy everything is created. The energy your body is created from is the same as that of a mountain. This energy unites the Universe. The conclusion is that underlying all matter, in all forms, is energy. This energy vibrates at different rates, and it is because of this that a rock is more solid and dense than a human body. Everything is formed from one energy source. Everything in the Universe is created from one source, whether they are animate or inanimate are connected. This means that we are constantly interacting with and influencing each other as though we were one gigantic body.

However, your frequency is different from other things in the Universe, hence it seems like you are separated from what you see around you – people, animals, plants, trees and so on. BUT you are not separated, you are in fact living in an ocean of energy, we all are. We are all connected at the lowest level which is called the unified field.

Vibrational frequency is the rate at which atoms and sub-particles of a being vibrate. The higher this vibrational frequency is, the closer it is to the frequency of light. Your words and thoughts send out a vibration that attracts an experience of a similar vibration. If you send out fear, you attract fear. If you send out love, you attract love. Everything has its own vibrational frequency. The table, the car, the picture frame, the rock, and even our thoughts and feelings, are all governed by the Law of Vibration. A table may look solid and still, but within the table are millions of sub-atomic particles "running around" and "popping" with energy. The table is pure energy and movement. Everything in this Universe has its own vibrational frequency. It is this Law of Vibration in action. However, we can't see it so it appears separate and solid to us. It is actually an illusion, making the Law of Vibration real. Even if you can't see it, it does not mean that it is not true.

The Law of Vibration states that all matter, thoughts, and feelings have their own vibrational frequency. The thoughts, feelings, and actions we choose also have their own particular rates of vibration. These vibrations will set up resonance with whatever possesses identical frequency. In other words, your thoughts are inseparably connected to the rest of the Universe. "Like attracts like." As you choose good thoughts, more good thoughts of alike nature will follow and you will also be in vibrational harmony with others with like thoughts.

Science, through Quantum Physics is showing us that everything in our Universe is energy, and energy vibrates at different rates. When we go down on a sub-atomic level we do not find matter, but pure energy. While others talk about this being the unified field or matrix, there is also talk about it being pure potentiality. You have a unique vibration, which is the product of all of the influences you have encountered. The influences you focus your attention on are those which determine your vibration. Negative vibrations are associated with the lower chakras. Negative vibrations include hatred, anger, doubt, fear, jealousy, envy, judgment, impatience, disharmony, imbalance, and insecurity. Positive vibrations are love, harmony, peace, balance, kindness, understanding, and compassion. The negative emotions are not bad. We must allow the energy of these lower vibrations to move through us and then with love let them go. We all, at one, time or another, experience emotions of a lower vibration. These emotions only become harmful when we base our words or actions upon them. You can feel anger about something and still make a conscious choice to act out of love. When you do this, you are raising your vibration from one of anger to one of love. Changing your thoughts and actions will help raise your vibrational frequency.

Before the invention of the microscope, people would have labeled you totally crazy if you told them that small "creatures crawled around" on the skin of all human beings. Humans live by the old saying "seeing is believing," but why do we not learn from history and realize that something might be true even though we do not see it. We do not need to see something to believe it.

It should be the other way around which is "believing will make you see." Most people only choose to look at what they know now and what they can see. They only rely on their five senses, and are unwilling to accept that everything vibrates and that the Law of Vibration is real. That we are vibrating sending towers transmitting our thoughts and feelings into the Universe all the time. Most people are only looking inside their frame of knowledge. In other words, they only relate to what they can see, verify and test. They rely on their five senses to tell them what their reality is. They are only using their sensory level to define their frame of knowledge in the time we are living. This frame however seems to change when science can tell us that something is true. Before it was a "fact" that the earth was flat, but as we know now it wasn't, it is round. Then the earth was the center of the Universe, but it wasn't. Then the Milky Way was the only galaxy, but it wasn't. It was only one of billions of galaxies. Our frame of knowledge is constantly changing since science is showing us "new" truths. Our frame of knowledge has been changing as long as we have lived on this planet. It is about time that we realized that something can be a reality even though we can't use our five senses to verify it. The dog whistle is a good example to illustrate a point about what we perceive as true or not. Today, we all know that dogs can detect sounds that are undetectable to the human ear. When someone blows a dog whistle we send out positive thoughts and vibrations as part of their behavior. We need to believe that everything is possible. We just need to believe it. Believing is seeing.

Our thoughts are on a certain vibrational frequency and hence are part of the vibrating Universe. The Law of

Attraction, which is based on the Law of Vibration states that we attract what we are sending out. Hence positive energies attract positive energies, and negative energies attract negative energies. Our thoughts are cosmic waves of energy that penetrate all time and space. Thought is the most potent vibration so this means that you can attract to what you want and wish for.

Albert Einstein said, "Everything is Vibration." But if this is true, if everything is just a form of energy vibration, then there should be a process where new vibrations come into existence and others cease to exist. Also, this process should be able to explain why we all have a future that is always uncertain and interactive relative to our actions, with a past that is always unchangeable and only really existing as a memory in the mind of the individual. Such a process has to be a physical continuum that is unfolding at the smallest unit of vibrational energy, the light quanta of quantum physics. Therefore it is unfolding photon oscillations which in turn forms a great dance of energy exchange, with new photon oscillations continuously coming into existence. I believe we see and feel this process as the continuum of time itself. Many people have said that "time" cannot be explained as a physical process, but there is disagreement with this because of all the hard work that has been done, and only a new interpretation has to be put forward. At the level of the atoms, this process has been explained by quantum mechanics. And at the level of our everyday life, the photon oscillations are the carrier of the electromagnetic force with the movement of EM fields and the flow of electric charge, which has been explained by Michael Faraday and others. The interactive part of this process has been explained by the interactive geometry of Einstein's theories on relativity.

This theory explains the outward momentum of light which forms the forward flow of time within each individual reference frame. This happens because light is a wave until it comes in contact with the electrons of an atom. When it does this, it will form a photon electron coupling representing a new moment in time with matter, anti-matter being the process that annihilates the past. Matter is the form of electrons that are continuously interacting with light forming a new probability wave function of future possibilities. Therefore we have a continuous renewing process forming the future photon by photon.

On the scale of our everyday life, this will form the movement of EM fields with electrical potential representing our own future potential within our own reference frame. We have a Universe of electrical potential of continuous creations continuously coming into existence photon by photon with the flow of EM fields within an infinite number of reference frames. This is a Universal process from the largest object to the smallest creature which will all create their own reference frame. Even as you respond to this comment, your action will be relative to the electrical activity in your brain within your own created reference frame.

Life is vibration, so is mind, and so is matter. Electricity or vibration is that same power we call the Creative Force. As the electrical vibrations are given, know that life itself, to be sure, is the Creative Force, yet its manifestations in man are electrical or vibratory. Electricity is the Creative Force in action! Seeing this, feeling this, knowing this, we find not only does the body become revivified, but by the creating in every atom of its being the knowledge of the activity of this Creative Force or principle as related to spirit, mind, body, all three are renewed.

We each have our own vibrations, and vibrate at our own rate. Vibrations vary in intensity within each person and from person to person, depending upon the experiences being manifested. We are attuned to our vibrations and this attunement is acted upon or varied by the forces surrounding us or within us. It would seem that vibrations act as a cohesive agent in all nature holding things together as all force is vibration.

All bodies radiate those vibrations with which it, the body controls itself, in mental and physical, and such radiation is called the aura. Akashic Records hold the radiations that an entity leaves behind. Plasmas that have to do with coagulations are positive, pollens are negative. Each functioning organ of the sensory system reflects a different vibration.

If and when our bodies deviate from their natural vibration, disease and ill effects can occur. To begin to understand what vibrational energy can really do for you, it helps to realize that the human body is really a magnificent quantum physics machine. We are made up of literally nothing more than vibrating energy. Humans are made of cells, which are made of atoms, which are made of particles, and those so-called particles are actually just vibrating energy. Every atom is just a probability wave, and most of the stuff we call physical matter is really made up of completely empty space. We are more empty space than physical stuff, more vibration than mass. Thus, we can be strongly impacted either positively or negatively by vibrational energy. Ultraviolet radiation from the sun for example, helps support healthy moods, brain function, endocrine system function and sleep cycles. Sunlight photons also help us generate Vitamin D, which prevents cancer, diabetes, depression and bone loss. Infrared

14

radiation has been proven to speed recovery of wounds and injuries, and infrared LED devices are being tested by NASA to speed the growth of plants in space. With modern society bombarding us with so much electromagnetic energy, it seems increasingly obvious that getting more in tune with the Earth Energy is a basis for healing. People who leave big, noisy cities and move out to the country enjoy spectacular health improvements. People who contact the earth through gardening, outdoor activities, or consuming natural foods are far healthier than those who don't. And, almost everyone agrees that a lush, green forest humming with life is calming and healing to both the mind and body. One explanation behind all this is that the Earth itself hums at a specific frequency, well below the audible detection range of human beings, called the Schumann frequency or Schumann resonance. If you multiply this Schumann resonance by multiples of two, you get higher harmonics of the same frequency, sort of like a higher octave on the piano. You can have a low level C note or a high level C note, and if you play them together, they are in harmony even though one is an octave higher than the other.

If you want to help people get in touch with the frequency of the Earth, the best thing to do is get them vibrating at multiples of the Earth frequency. Through a process called entrainment, physical objects absorb the vibrational frequencies of their immediate surroundings. If you have two tuning forks and you knock one of them to get it vibrating, you only have to hold it near the other tuning fork for it to start vibrating too. The vibration frequency radiates from the source to all objects around it, causing these objects to vibrate in harmony with this source. This is essentially what the portable Rife and the MWO machines do as well. These machines broadcast a high energy healing frequency, entraining your mind, body, and even the physical space around you to a frequency that's more in tune with healthy vibration.

Energy in a pure sense without Newtonian restrictions, is a global term that we use to describe a form of existence that we cannot perceive with our standard senses but know that it does exist. In other words, we are using energy to describe differences that we sense within our ability of physical measure at this time. This is also used to describe forces of information that is perceived as beyond the electromagnetic spectrum.

We as human vessels made of earth material, work together as receptor sites for the earth to gain information about its surface and the Universe. Since we are able to hold and transmute energy, when we ground ourselves we then become a stronger conduit as we can then pass more information/ energy/light through our nervous system to the earth giving it a greater experience of its own self. Different people work like different sensory organs for the body of the earth, to pick up and sense different ranges within the electromagnetic spectrum itself. Similar to olfactory nerves that work for smell, vestibular nerves that work for balance, cochlear nerves that work for hearing, rods and cones that work for light, (these are examples of different organs working to pick up specific ranges within one electromagnetic spectrum). We choose to perceive them as being separate ranges and making them different experiences, but they are different frequencies within a larger spectrum of existence.

We are those receptors for the planet and if we do not connect, the planet does not fully know and is unable to coordinate the orchestra of energy that makes up its surface. When enough of us disconnect from the planet, we become like a cancer to the earth as we do what we think is correct and best without higher guidance. But when you ground and reconnect stronger to the planet, you gain a greater understanding and direction as the planet directs you towards your greatest purpose here. With that new understanding, you then change your behavior to better match both your purpose and the planets needs with a joyful heart. At that point, you are technically in remission in cancer terms.

Chapter 2

The Differences between Vibration and Frequency

If we want to understand how the material world is created and what keeps it in a perpetual state of motion, we need to study the language of the living energy codes of matter, which is made of light, sound, frequency, and vibration. Most of us know that the material world is made of matter, but we do not understand the mechanics behind it. Conventional Science taught us that the material world came into existence by accident. If we study the science of matter deeply enough, we should eventually come to the conclusion that the material world did not occur by accident. The fact that physics can describe the Universe using only mathematical formulas is proof that a divine being designed and created the material or external world. These formulas were not created by scientists, rather they were rediscovered.

As you experience it yourself, you experience that the entire material world is nothing but vibration. When we experience the ocean of infinite waves surging within, the river of inner sensations flowing within, the eternal dance of the countless vibrations within every atom of the body, we will witness our continuously changing nature. All of this is happening at an extremely subtle level, as you experience the reality of matter to be vibration, you also start experiencing the reality of the mind, which is consciousness, perception, sensation, and reaction.

Nurturing yourself raises your vibration and sends a signal of Love into the Universe.

The Law of Nature states that everything has a vibration. If you've taken a chemistry class you probably remember learning about atoms, and that everything is made up of atoms. These atoms are in a constant state of motion and depending on the speed of these atoms, things either appear as a solid, liquid, or a gas. Sound is also a vibration, and so are our thoughts.

Everything that manifests itself in your life is there because it matches the vibration from your thoughts. Vibration refers to movement and vibrations are measured by the frequency per second. Touch, sound, odour, taste, and sight are each characterized by particular ranges of vibrations, and all phenomena perceived by these senses occur within defined ranges of vibration.

Colors have meaning and they are vibrations in the visible spectrum. These locations are also in direct relation to the major chakras, while their vibrancy shades and extent, is in relation to the activity of the particular chakras.

When we look at vibration and frequency from the perspective of the external creation, vibration and frequency have their differences. In physics, vibration is the "oscillating, reciprocating, or other periodic motion of a rigid or elastic body or medium forced from a position or state of equilibrium." As for oscillation, it is "an effect expressible as a quantity that repeatedly and regularly fluctuates above and below some mean value, as the pressure of a sound wave or the voltage of an alternating current." In simple words, it is a motion that repeats itself. Frequency is the cyclic pattern of scalar waves that flash "on" and "off." The vibrational frequency rate is determined by how fast energy units (partiki) contract and expand. In physics, frequency is the number of waves that pass a fixed point in unit time. Partiki units are the smallest building blocks of matter, even smaller than the smallest particles known to scientists. Partiki is made of units of conscious energy that act like the template upon which consciousness enters manifestation.

In certain spiritual teachings of energy mechanics, the process when energy contracts toward the neutral point is known as vibration, and the process when energy expands away from the neutral point is known as oscillation. The combination of vibration and oscillation is what determines the vibrational frequency rate (cyclic pattern of scalar waves) of all things. Scalar waves are standing waves that flash "on" and "off." This process creates energy patterns that are processed by our consciousness and DNA to create our external reality. The on and off energy pattern is very simple but yet it has infinite potential. This is the mysterious and amazing power of the intelligence of creation.

The core structures of reality work similar to how a computer works. A computer communicates and operates through the use of binary codes, which are codes that consist of ones (on) and zeros (off). Binary codes are very simple but with the right combinations they can help computers create magnificent things. For example, when we paint a picture using a computer software, the core state of the colors and shapes in the pictures are basically made of ones and zeros. We do not see our picture as ones and zeros, because the central processing unit (CPU) and its counterparts process the binary codes as colors and shapes. The greatest thing about binary codes is that there are no limits to their combinations.

To further understand how binary codes work, binary codes work by representing content (letters, symbols, colors) in a form that computers can understand. This is done by breaking the content into a numeric system of two digits "0" and "1." To accomplish this, computers use electrical impulses switching OFF and ON to represent these two digit numbers.

This can be better understood by understanding how a computer chip works.

A computer chip is made of millions of transistors that act as switches much like a light bulb in your home. If you want light you move the switch to "on" to allow electricity to flow through the light bulb thus giving you light, but if you switch back to "off" the light goes away because the electrical signal is interrupted. The switching behavior from a computer chip is similar in the sense that it can only understand two results, "on" and "off." These results correspond well with the two digits numeric systems of "1" and "0" best described as binary ("1" representing "on" and "O" representing "off").

The simple process of using binary codes to create things within the hardware of computers is very similar to how Creation creates our eternal reality or material world. The material world works very similar to a virtual reality. At its core, the material world is made of only light (energy) that flashes on and off to create energy codes. This fundamental process that involves light flashing on and off is known as "partiki phasing." Partiki phasing creates energy patterns, which are then processed by our consciousness and DNA before we become aware of our existence in the material world. It is at this moment that we are tricked into believing that our reality is made of solid material. In reality, the material world is made of only energy patterns. This is the big secret of the Art of Creation. Partiki are responsible for creating our external reality. It is through the dynamics of their interaction that electromagnetic fields of sound frequency, and light spectra are created, and frequency and vibration are brought into being. Vibration and frequency play very important roles in creating the structure of matter because they help organize matter, giving it appearances, and uniqueness. For this reason, vibration and frequency are essential for life to exist. Vibration and frequency organize matter into sacred geometries and shapes. Sacred geometries are some of the building blocks of matter and therefore without them reality cannot exist.

Frequencies, Sound + Vibration = Sacred Geometry

To further explain that there is no solidity to the Universe, a form that appears solid is actually created by an underlying vibration. Vibrations express themselves in corresponding geometrical figures and in this way build up crystals that are the expression of vibration. Crystals collectively form a body of an element according to its particular vibration. The forms of snowflakes and faces of flowers take on their shape because they are responding to some sound in nature. Crystals, plants, and human beings are music that has taken on a visible form.

Scatter some very fine sand over the head of a drum. Then take a tuning fork and strike a note just above the drum head causing it to vibrate. The sand would shift and assume a geometrical figure corresponding to the particular note that was played. When another is sounded, the sand will shift and assume another figure. This shows that every vibration produces a corresponding geometric form. Matter is a projection of energy and therefore it behaves more like an illusion. Vibration and Frequency allow light and sound to have expression, giving them unique properties and characteristics. When we remember Einstein's famous equation e=mc2, we are aware that everything in this Universe is energy. All particles however small or large are energy masquerading as everything from strings, quarks, protons, electrons, atoms, planets, solar systems, galaxies to Universes. We know that light or photons travel from stars and when put through a glass prism we can see the spectrum of colors within the light. The prism bends the light and the colors represent the different frequencies of energy. Frequencies move like waves in an ocean – up and down repeating cyclically. So light is made up of energy vibrating and oscillating within a very tight range frequency. Sound also travels in waves of frequencies, but sound waves are much larger than light waves and need some kind of matter to travel upon.

Vibration and frequency are two factors that combine as principles of existence within the electromagnetic spectrum as it describes propagation and spatial existence respectively. They are closely related but do not describe the same thing. Frequency is describing a wave propagation through space with peaks and valleys in a scalar fashion through space, which means that it holds the same nodes and nulls through all forms of space. Space is timeless and Time is constructed based on our movement through space. That is all part of two other factors which are vibration and oscillation which make up the creation of the vibrational frequency rate (cycling waveform of a scalar wave). Vibration is the movement of contracting energy towards a neutral point, a point without motion and thus no time. On the other side of awareness is the motion of oscillation which is expanding energy away from the neutral point, thus speeding time up.

If you look at our modern scientific representation of a standing wave form it will always be of a position in relation to time, as that is our agreed upon reference. If you take time away as a reference and simply plotted positional changes in space and where they occurred, you would have nothing more than a dot, as all positions would be the same and we would no longer be moving to compare a change. Since we are moving very quickly through space on a large planet, our reference is the same here but different in the Universal space of reality. Every positional change in the Universe brings a different energetic mixing of frequencies and non-frequency based information to create a new Heterodyne Frequency that beats into existence our reality. If all movements truly stopped in all their forms, then we would be one Universal energy beating as one. If that happened then we would not be here to have a unique experience and grow within ourselves a greater awareness of one specific aspect of the reality that the Creator has created.

In closing, there is agreement among science, medicine, and metaphysics that certain frequencies can repel disease, and certain frequencies can destroy disease. Herein lies the link between frequency (vibration) and health. Scientific research has shown that different parts of our bodies have their own sonic signature. In other words, the sound of the cells of your heart differs from the sound of the cells of your lungs.

When parts of the body become stressed or dis-eased, they are no longer producing the correct sound wave. Simply put, they are not vibrating at their prime (optimal) resonant frequency. To re-establish or recalibrate your frequency, you need to understand how lower and higher vibrations affect your energy and health.

Chapter 3

The Three Types of Energy in the Universe

Your own energy field is called your Mer-Ka-Ba. The Mer-Ka-Ba is alive and responds only to the conscious intentions of the spirit within the field. Energy fields are present around the human body and are created by the movement of energy and consciousness within the chakras.

There are three types of energies or forces of the Universe that are important to our understanding because we live in an energy-manifested world. These three types of energies are:

Fohat – Fohat manifests as universal physical forces; motion, gravity, electricity, magnetism, sound, heat, chemical reactions, radiation, etc. These physical forces are convertible, one into another. Fohat is the primordial force of vitality in the cosmos. It is that which links spirit and matter in the first stages of differentiation. In the manifested stages of the Universe, fohat is the force that causes the differentiation from the one to the many, while at the same time, it is the power that unites and combines the various units and atoms of the cosmos.

Fohat can be described as "cosmic vitality" or the prana of the Universe. It has been considered as the universal energy which includes all the forces of nature. It is the energizing force of the Universe. Force is often seen as blind energy, but Fohat is not by any means blind, but a directed and intelligent power, or in other words, power imbued with purpose.

Fohat is a power in a dynamic form and is the creative purpose flowing through the manifested universe, but it can, in contrast to "creativity," manifest as a fierce destructive force. Thus it can be regarded as duality, Fohat being both the active "male" potency and Sakti (female), the reproductive power in nature. This duality has been likened to the function of a seal and wax.

Sakti is the capacity to take up an impression, inherent in wax and in other plastic and pliant materials, while Fohat is the potency that makes the impression, the seal, stamp or dye itself, imprinting a replica of its own characteristics upon the receptive wax. Both Fohat and Sakti represent differentiations of the larger universal Fohat as the Once Force.

It is possible to picture Fohat on a wide scale as a dynamic pulsating energy, not unlike electricity, but not identified with it. Unlike electricity, Fohat has rather been seen as some vast and cosmic consciousness operating at every "level" of the cosmos and linking each plane to the other; spirit to mind and mind to matter. In such a sense Fohat might be described as the "law-giver" of the Universe.

It is necessary to briefly outline, as clearly as possible,

a picture of how Fohat manifests and works, keeping in mind the fact that it is not that which manifests, but the invisible energy behind that manifested form. In the mineral kingdom Fohat emerges as such phenomena as electricity although the actual work done by electricity is by virtue of the movement of electrons. It also appears on the material level as prana where it organizes matter as living material.

Prana or Etheric Field – Prana manifests as universal life force, breathing life into being and breathing out in the fundamental rhythm we experience as life and death. It is the energy that gives life to the body and all its parts, providing structure, and holding the physical molecules and cells together as organs and in relationship to each other. Prana exists at all levels and animates all the bodies composing the whole person. Although it comes out of the whole body, it is seen primarily around your hands, feet, head, and a slight bit on your shoulders as well. It emanates as a soft, white-blue light. Immediately next to the skin is a black field, and just beyond it begins a light bluish light. This bluish light is the prana or the life-force energy of your body. If it's around your hands, it'll show up anywhere from a quarter inch to maybe three or four inches away, but around the rest of your body it usually extends less than an inch from the skin.

In addition, beyond the prana field, as it radiates away from the body, is another field of energy that is not associated directly with your breath, but with your thoughts and emotions. Your thoughts emit electromagnetic fields from your brain, and your emotions also put out electromagnetic fields. You can see them, they are visible and this field of energy is called our auric field. However, most people have tuned this auric field out in themselves and others so they don't know that it is there.

Cameras have now been connected to computers that can photograph the aura, so it is no longer guesswork, but a scientific fact. Cells develop into nerve fibre, and prana pulsates through these fibres.

Prana is also the life force emanating from the sun as vitality absorbed from the air we breathe and the food we eat.

Kundalini – Kundalini manifests as a transforming force centered in the base chakra, operating within the body and driving evolution, desire, sex drive, growth, and individual development. It exists on all planes in seven degrees of force. Kundalini is a Sanskrit term from ancient India that identifies the arising of an energy and consciousness which has been coiled at the base of the spine since birth, and is the source of the life force (pranic energy, chi, bio-energy) that everybody knows. Yogic science suggests that this energy triggered the formation of the child in the womb, and then coils 3 ½ times at the base of the spine to hold the energy field in stasis until we die, when it uncoils and returns to its source. Kundalini may unravel and arise from the base of the spine (or sometimes from the feet) due to spiritual practices, or in response to life events, and when this happens it may move gradually, uncoiling like a snake, or quickly and explosively, into the gut, the heart or the head. This event can be startling and chaotic, frightening or blissful, and it usually triggers months and years of new sensations and changes in the person who awakens it. It may feel like the body's wiring has moved from 110 to 220, and it takes time to adapt to it. It is understood in the eastern tradition to be a significant adjunct to spiritual realization, but it is rarely recognized as such in western traditions, although Christian mystics have often been said to have intense energetic or physical problems. Kundalini awakening can trigger a wide range of phenomena, both positive and negative. It can cause significant changes in the physical, emotional, sensate and psychic capacities, cause stress in vulnerable areas of the body, open the heart and mind to major shifts in perspective, and cause many unique and unfamiliar sensations including shaking, vibrating, spontaneous movement, visions, and many other phenomena.

Kundalini awakening offers a profound opportunity for those called to follow a spiritual path. It gradually releases many patterns, conditions and delusions of the separate self. It can be threatening to the ego-structure because a person may feel a loss of interest in their old life and identity, and consciousness may go into unfamiliar expansive or empty states that are disorienting. It also makes people who are unfamiliar with it afraid they are ill or losing their minds so understanding it is important.

Like any energy or creation (prana, electricity, atoms) this energy can be activated and misused by those who are not spiritually motivated or have not completed this process and are therefore not free of personal patterns. It is very helpful to understand the process and the intention of your own life force as it awakens you so that you may discover wisdom, love and authentic direction in your own life. Simplicity, contentment, unconditional acceptance and presence are hallmarks of an awakened life.

Chapter 4

Understanding and Transmitting Energy

In order to protect ourselves from negative energy or people, and to know what we need to do to truly take care of ourselves, regardless of your environment, it is essential to bring more consciousness into your life.

If you cannot be present in normal circumstances, such as when you are sitting alone in a room, walking in the woods, or listening to someone, then you certainly won't be able to stay conscious when something goes wrong or you are faced with difficult people or situations, with loss or the threat of loss. You will be taken over by a reaction, which ultimately is always some form of fear, and pulled into deep consciousness. These challenges are your tests. Only the way in which you deal with them will show you and others where you are at as far as your state of consciousness is concerned, not how long you can sit with your eyes closed or what visions you see.

So, it is essential to bring more consciousness into your life in ordinary situations when everything is going relatively smoothly. In this way, you grow in presence power. It generates an energy field in you and around you of a high vibrational frequency. No unconsciousness, no negativity, no discord or violence can enter that field and survive, just as darkness cannot survive in the presence of light. Our thoughts are also very powerful and help to create a high vibration energy field in and around us. The entire material world is nothing but vibration. Sound is a vibration, and so are our thoughts. Everything that manifests itself in your life is there because it matches the vibration from your thoughts.

For us, thought is where it all begins. As your conscious

mind dwells habitually on thoughts of a certain quality, these become firmly imbedded within the subconscious mind. They become the dominant vibration and this dominant vibration sets up a resonance with other similar vibrations and draws them into your life. This is easier to understand if you consider that from the metaphysical view, the whole Universe is MIND. In turn, your vibrations affect everything around you – your environment, the people and animals around you, the inanimate objects, even the seemingly 'empty space' and they, in turn, affect you.

Your feelings at the present moment dictate your vibration. It is said that feeling is a word to define conscious awareness of a vibration. So, your feeling at the moment is your vibration you are in which sets up things of like nature. Positive feelings = positive circumstances, negative feelings = negative circumstances.

We live in a Universe of spiritual, psychic, and physical energy by virtue when all living things exist through their ability to transmute this Universal energy into something individual. We become endowed with the ability to transmit our own energy field, our individual unit of power. Humans are energy transformers; we are alive and developing in proportion to how much of this Universal energy we accept and how freely it flows through us. The better we transmit this energy or allow it to flow through us, the higher grade we occupy; the more alive and contented and effective we become.

Frederic W.H. Myers (1843 – 1901 CE), an early investigator of spiritual and psychic energy, conceived of the subliminal self as being in touch with a realm of spiritual forces from which it is able to draw energy to infuse into the human mind, ordinarily in limited quantities, but, in altered states, in great floods, which elevate the mental operations and powers to exceptionally high levels.

Myers viewed the brain as being at a comparatively early stage in its evolution as an instrument through which the higher self operates in the material world. He conceived of the subliminal self as that part of the Higher Self (soul) which remains unexpressed in our conscious and organic life. The subliminal self surpasses the supraliminal (above the threshold of consciousness) or ordinary conscious self in its range of spiritual and psychic powers.

Our personal energy convergence point is a center of reception and radiation at the same time. The energy waves from the one Quintessence sustain us and are manifested in our separate frequency transmission. Our individual essence maintains itself by passing Higher Energy pulsations through it. The instant when the Higher Energy flows through us is our moment of absolute unity with the divinity. The individual power which occasions the flow through of Higher Energy is composed of sureness of our belief in the existence of this greater force.

Preserving and Storing Energy – The Universe is a web of energy conveying life force through its emanations. All entities within this network receive and transmit energy through radiations. A unitive experience of spiritual, psychic, and physical energy occurs as a direct response to the impelling force we create within ourselves. Whatever integration we achieve results in the issuing forth of energy from a higher dimension in direct proportion to our self-invigoration. We receive and transmit spiritual, psychic, and physical energy in immediate relation to our developing intellectual and spiritual capability. We learn to attune ourselves to the Universal energy frequency, experiencing spiritual and psychic entrainment.

The energy we conduct of the Higher Force calls its complement into our being. Emanations of Higher Energy become available to transform our lives, recharging and repairing our own systems. Energy upheavals shift us out of destructive habits, encouraging us to relearn integrative ways of being.

Sexual/Creative Energy – Sexual energy is your creative energy and it is vitally important to use that time with the energy, to express your creativity. This can be done through movement, building, designing, painting, and more specifically tackling things that would be normally perceived as a barrier or outside yourself.

The energy is already a part of you, so there is nothing to be added, gained, or lost by focusing on using this energy. Say thank-you and start the movement of your deepest expressions of vibration coming out naturally, from working with this energy. Take one action to start the creating process in motion, and then bring your thoughts into reality. Sexual/Creative Energy is a specific type of energetic expression and pulse emitted by the body; it is also associated with your C2 Chakra. If you learn to direct sexual energy towards a creative means, you will amplify the creative process to your maximum ability. It becomes amplified in groups and creativity jumps exponentially, and the same occurs in all forms of energetic expression and thought.

Energetic Patterns – Energetic patterns exist in all of us and bring into our awareness the emotions that need to be integrated, otherwise they would no longer be there. For example, we do not need to be in the energy of abuse, but the fact that we had the energetic expression and reaction means that we need to bring in, feel, and accept the emotion for its wonderful expression. As human beings, we will continue to repeat a particular emotional state over and over again until we finally realize and learn what it is we are looking for with that expressed emotional state in our life. Now, every time we repeat the emotion we get a small physiological expression of that emotion. If we repeat that emotion, our body will create or grow cells in response to make that expression easier for us, as we apparently want to stay in that state of expression more frequently during the day.

Lastly and very importantly, let it all go and every attachment we have with it, or associated with it. Let all the energy go and flow where it is needed and wanted. Imagining and feeling the energy of expression rooting and merging with you is very helpful. Then, let it go with a fire that burns from working, getting progressively larger with your vision, followed by a long, peaceful breath where you release all attachments and by-products that you may feel. Love the energy and let it go, or love it and let it go.

The same thing happens when we grow extra skin cells in response to a physical stimulus that we repeat, such as calluses on your hands from gardening, work related tasks, on the side of your toe from bunions, or any other repeated irritation.

If we die and go to heaven living forever in a state of communion, and knowing of and about one another we will automatically know what another needs and exactly how to help them in every moment of expression. With a knowing like that, there would no longer be a novel expression of the unknown creating a new or different emotional response. By coming here and forgetting everything that you once knew, you allow for novel expressions of the emotional range of vibration in its purest form. With this awareness we can gain a much deeper knowing and wisdom related to that expression. For example, by expressing emotion without understanding or connectedness we gain a new insight into the expression of compassion.

If you knew that you chose the reality that you were living in, then you would be far less compassionate towards another person or persons because you would know that they are the only ones to choose another reality and to start expressing it. Why would you feel sorry for another if their only way in and out of a living reality was by their own choices and nobody else's.

There are centers of energy physically and spiritually associated with various parts of our bodies, called chakras. When kundalini energy moves through the various chakras, our consciousness necessarily changes with it. Each chakra is said to correspond to a specific mantra (sound) and geometric pattern (yantra). Through meditation on these chakras it is claimed that we can gain mastery over our body and each corresponding element.

Chakras have no physical reality. They are vortexes of consciousness forming a kind of "management system" that transforms energies to meet the needs of the evolving body-mind-spirit complex operating as a human entity. Also, chakras do not function in isolation from one another but are part of a system of energy flowing between them.

The chakras are the energy centers of the body, and are often referred to as our "spiritual batteries." Our anatomy is a complex piece of engineering served by a network of etheric wiring through which energy flows. The chakras are the organizing centers that act as both reception and transmission points for important information and life energies (chi/prana), which are essential for the well-being of our body, mind, and continuation of our spiritual development.

The original undifferentiated energy from creation is often called Akasha in Indian philosophy and modern occult circles. In some embodiments of the Perennial Tradition – "a perspective in the philosophy of religion which views each of the world's religious traditions as sharing a single, universal truth from which all esoteric and exoteric knowledge and doctrine has grown," it is termed the Secret Fire.

This elemental psychic energy is completely instinctual and unconscious and is heavily influenced by spiritual, psychic, and psychological phenomena. One of the major functions of the Secret Fire is to increase human self-awareness. At the lowest level, this is the ego, at its highest, it is the higher self. In the vast majority of humanity, this Secret Fire, or liberating energy of self-consciousness, is said to lie dormant at the base of the spine, coiled like a serpent. By learning to contact the various focal points of energy, what are called the chakras, the person moves the focus of consciousness into the various areas. If the Secret Fire reaches the top of the skull and beyond, spiritual awakening can occur, allowing for a descent and re-ascent of the energy, during which the psychic centers can be awakened, allowing for the manifestation of psychic powers and related phenomena.

The Secret Fire is directly linked to sexual and creative forces in humans. Sexual desire can act as one of the basic evolutionary impulses, along with Higher Intellectual forces.

The dormant capability and need for positive orgasmic experiences is biologically and psychologically rooted. Sexual experience within the context of genuine love involves experience of spiritual transcendence, foreshadowing ecstatic union with the One. The "little death" or petite morte of the sexual orgasm, is a forerunner of the "big death" as we let and experience divine oblivion.

Psychological Interpretations of Psychic Energy – Theorists such as Sigmund Freud and researchers such as Wilhelm Reich studied psychic energy from a psychological perspective, viewing it as a complex mental, sexual or libidinous energy in our unconscious. Psychological afflictions were said to be the result of blockage of psychic energy.

According to Freud, all behavior is motivated by the desire to feel pleasure. That motivation is organized and directed by two instincts: sexuality (EROS), and aggression (THANATOS). Freud conceptualized both these instincts as being powered by a form of internal psychic energy that he called the libido, a basic psychic energy.

Freud believed that humans must subordinate their desire for pleasure, primarily sexual in nature, to the reality principle:

the demand to live in conformity with socially concocted dictates, such as the subordination of women and children to a domineering, abusive father. Life thus becomes a joyless compromise with dysfunctional rules.

As we've seen, the sexual drive can be used in positive ways within the context of a mature love relationship. In most persons in contemporary society, however, the libidinous drives are thwarted or corrupted, resulting in psychological disorders of one form or another.

Freud's psychoanalytic techniques, a silent therapist listening to the free associations and dreams of the patient, was a gigantic fraud resulting in person's becoming more miserable rather than more functional.

Other psychologists and psychiatrists such as Wilhelm Reich and Erich Fromm saw the absurdity and devastation of counterfeit therapies, such as orthodox psychoanalysis, and developed new approaches to freeing psychic energy from social and personal obstructions and debasements. Reich's and Fromm's psychotherapeutic practices were positive in their effects, unlike Freud's. However, these approaches to relieving psychological and spiritual disorders operate entirely within the physical or psychic sphere, not in the spiritual domain.

Perennialist Procedures – Just as our current civilization uses various energy forms such as electricity, magnetism, and electromagnetic waves, prophets within the Perennial Tradition preserve and use spiritual energy. This more subtle form of energy operates according to specific principles which it is essential to learn and practice. Just as electricity is potentially deadly if handled by a person ignorant of its power, spiritual energy can be lethal if trifled with by the spiritually illiterate. Spiritual energy can be directed by concentrated meditation, which is how prayer and spiritual healing work. Perennialist meditation focuses and transmits spiritual energy, directing it to a specific destination for a specific purpose. Since external and internal energy focal points affect our bodies, minds, and states of consciousness so directly, we must carefully select the inputs we allow into our experience: persons, activities, images, thoughts, feelings, food, sounds, written material, and environmental elements.

Every time we interact with another person, there is an exchange of energy resonance. Extensive interaction with people possessing negative energy fields may debilitate us and leave us with a tremendous amount of harmful energy debris. Unless we learn to recognize negative energy and cleanse our fields of it, we can suffer physical, emotional, mental, and spiritual problems. Fortunately, the opposite is equally true: spending time with positively charged persons and edifying phenomena such as enlightening music, art, and literature, can bring transformative effects.

Our spiritual and psychic energy can be misused or wasted in a number of ways. Negative mental and emotional states allow for leakage of energy at a rapid pace (as if we punctured a balloon with a pin, creating a hole and resulting in the balloon exploding).

One of our greatest enemies in this regard is self-importance. We allow ourselves to be weakened by feeling offended by the deeds and misdeeds of other people. Our self-importance requires that we spend most of our lives offended by someone.

Appropriate self-regard is certainly an important factor in any healthy perception of oneself, but what we're referring to is what might be called high self-importance and pomposity.

Perennialist savants teach students to overcome all aspects of what is called the "debilitating self," a major element of which is self-importance. Students are taught the proper procedures to preserve, store, and use spiritual and psychic energy. Initiates are taught to take strategic inventories of what they do, especially their non-essential behavioural patterns to determine what can and should be forfeited to save and store energy. Stored energy is used to transform oneself. It's first necessary to identify with our Higher Self and develop a moment to moment awareness of what's happening in our personal energy fields and the energy networks affecting us. We learn to notice how we feel around certain people and in certain situations, for example whether we feel energized or enervated. Power struggles are about "stealing" each other's energy. If you feel "drained" after having been with a specific person, you're probably "losing energy" to that person.

We develop the ability to observe our emotions and thoughts as they occur. If we come in contact with a person or idea face to face, or while watching movies or television, that regularly "pushes our buttons," we must learn to control our energy field so unconscious reactions don't wreak havoc in our emotional life.

The "Outer-Directional Energy Flow" Syndrome – This phenomenon is usually "seen" by us as the person being "self-conscious" or "self-important," to a greater or lesser degree. We sometimes say of such people that they're "full of themselves," "always on camera," or that they try to "charm" other people. What we mean is that their energy is flowing outward through their eyes to "see" what others are thinking and feeling about them, attempting to pull other persons energy toward them.

The "Outer-Directional Energy Flow" Syndrome is not

always present in mere show-offs. Such "constantly on stage," performers may or may not have an outer-directed optical energy flow. The outer-directional energy flow can be most easily seen when it occurs in connection with a person's eyes. However, the same uncontrolled energy discharge can transpire in relation to other dysfunctional behavioural phenomena such as irrepressible talking, ungoverned negative thinking, and uncurbed destructive actions.

The Perennial Tradition teaches how spiritual energy must be accumulated and preserved, then transmitted to persons, events, and objects in connection with specific goals set by the Higher Self. This requires that most of the time a person must be accumulating and preserving spiritual energy, not leaking it through self-importance, negative emotions, or destructive actions. In regard to optical energy flow, spiritual energy must be made to "flow backward" through the eyes.

In Perennialist teachings this is termed the "death of the senses. The energy flow in the thinker must be inward as well, and this is called the "death of the mind."

The teacher who provides the most illuminating explications of this teaching is Plato. Plato made it clear that the ultimate attainment of unitive consciousness is possible only through muesis (literally, closing of the eyes): turning away from external sense-data and discovering truth through an introspective process of contemplation and meditation.

In the Phaedo, Socrates (Plato) reveals the secret nature of philosophy. "I hold that the true votary of philosophy (the search for wisdom) is likely to be misunderstood by other men; they do not perceive that his whole practice is of death and dying... When the soul exists in herself, and is released from the body and the body is released from the soul, death, surely, is nothing else than this..."

If we would have pure knowledge of anything we must be quit of the body, the soul in herself must behold things in themselves; and then we shall attain the wisdom which we desire, and of which we say that we are lovers.

True philosophers are always occupied in the practice of dying. It is the actual practice of learning to leave the physical body and live in the spiritual body, which is called "dying." In order to get rid of self-indulgent sensuality we must put an end to the cause of self indulgence, the rushing out of the senses to seize and enjoy their objects. We must draw them back when they are inclined thus to rush out, draw them away from their objects, as the tortoise draws in his limbs into the shell, so these into their source, quiescent in the mind, the mind quiescent in intelligence, the intelligence quiescent in the soul, and its self-knowledge, observing the action of Nature, but not subject to it, not craving anything that the external life can give."

Sri Aurobindo, Essays on the Gita

Chapter 5

The Benefits of being in a High Vibration

Have you heard people talking about attaining a higher vibration? Are you unsure of what that means or why it's important to you?

We all vibrate energetically at a particular frequency. The lower the frequency, the denser your energy, and the heavier your problems seem. Here you may experience pain and discomfort in your physical body and experience heavy emotions and mental confusion. Psychically, your energy is darker and you need to exert a good deal of effort to accomplish your goals. Overall, your life takes on a negative quality.

The higher the frequency of your energy or vibration, the

lighter you feel in your physical, emotional, and mental bodies. You experience greater personal power, clarity, peace, love, and joy. You have little if any discomfort or pain in your physical body, and your emotions are easily dealt with. Your energy is literally full of light! Your life flows with synchronicity, and you manifest what you desire with ease. Overall, your life takes on a positive quality.

Being in a higher vibration is going to become more and more important to you and the rest of the world as we experience greater awareness of the polarities between the lower and higher vibrations. We will begin to perceive greater separation between the "dark" and "light" almost as if we live in two different worlds at once. We will need to consciously choose between the dark and the light or the higher and lower vibrations.

Despair and desperation due to challenges will consume

those vibrating at a lower frequency. Know that help is available from those vibrating at the higher frequency. The lower and denser energies will naturally want to rise when around the higher and lighter energies.

However, this process will feel very uncomfortable to people who carry the lower energies and people who carry the higher energies for a while. It is important for people who carry a higher vibration to maintain it and not lower it no matter how uncomfortable it feels. Those people resonating at a higher vibration will only be able to maintain it as long as they don't succumb to the pull of the lower vibration. That pull will come in the form of old programs and patterns of needing approval or of wanting to "fit in."

When you choose to be in a higher vibration, you are an example. Choosing the light of a higher vibration requires a firm commitment to it even when it feels as though you no longer fit in. You won't receive approval or fit in any longer because you **WILL** stand out from those with a lower vibration just as a tiny light in the midst of a dark room stands out. Understand that those with the lower vibration have the potential to raise their frequency. Remember that you will be able to find people who resonate at a higher vibration where you will have the support you need to keep your light shining bright.

Your vibration describes your overall state of being. Everything in the Universe is made up of energy vibrating at different frequencies. Even things that look solid are made up of vibrational energy fields at the quantum level and this includes you.

Everything physically manifested vibrates within certain ranges of frequency in order for our human senses to perceive it. Raising your vibration enables you to receive a more direct guidance and clearer guidance from your Higher Self because you are now vibrating at a higher rate. Having this direct link allows for information to be more easily accepted by the conscious and the actualized. Raising your vibration also opens you up to different levels of consciousness. Consequently, raising your vibration heightens your awareness, develops telepathy, intuition, and increases ESP abilities in which to live your life in a more conscious manner. This expanded awareness of energy also helps to open and develop channels of communication from other realms of Light Beings, Spirit Guides, and Nature Spirits. These realms encourage intuition, knowing, and the ability to receive evident guidance from Spirit, thus enhancing your quality of life by imbuing harmony, balance, joy, and inner peace.

Your reception of this increased Love or Light into your being projects itself into everything you do, effecting and anchoring more Light on the Earth plane. Furthermore, this benefits humanity by pioneering the path which will result in encouraging others to evolve on their spiritual path. By engaging in daily practices like mindfulness, meditation, daily affirmations, yoga, and healthy eating we shift our energy. Nurturing ourselves raises our vibration and sends a signal of Love into the Universe. We begin to operate at a high vibrational frequency, the frequency of Love, and that's when we are a magnet for more positive relationships and experiences.

When our energetic aura shifts, our consciousness expands, our nervous system neutralizes, and we begin to fully realize and experience a spiritual awakening, the recognition of our divine essence. Things become possible that weren't before. A miraculous life unfolds in front of us.

Raising your vibration happens through experience and

LIVING LIFE as "You want it to be," and then growing from everything that you experience. All experiences are good and there for you to grow in all forms which automatically raises your vibration. It needs no worry, or dread, or guilt, but a love for what has occurred in your life, in all experiences, yes all. Many people believe that things "just happen" to them, but as we connect more closely to our intuition we are shown that everything that happens to us is of our own creation. We may not be fully aware of what we are creating moment to moment, but fortunately the Universe provides us with many signs to let us know when we are on the right path, and more importantly when we are on the wrong path.

In general, warning signs from the Universe occur in the form of unwanted circumstances and events. The signs are an indication that your energy is headed towards or currently stuck in a low vibrational frequency. Your thoughts, feelings, and actions are focused negatively, and this is creating unwanted circumstances.

Conversely, when your thoughts, feelings, and actions are moving at a higher vibrational frequency, life will line up perfectly. You will have excellent timing and good luck all day long. This is why it's so important to raise your vibration by consciously choosing positive thoughts. Although we have the ability to resonate at a high vibrational frequency, it is challenging for us to stay elevated all the time.

This is because our souls are stuck here on Earth in a physical dimension that is much denser and slower than the higher, ethereal dimensions. The simple makeup of our planet and bodies is composed of much lower vibrational energy than that of our souls.

As a result, we will likely bump up against unwanted circumstances from time to time, but that's ok. As long as we heed these warning signs without allowing our egos to fixate on them, we can get back on track quickly. As you move through your day, it's a good idea to take note of the warning signs from the Universe. Here are a few examples of signs to be mindful of: stubbing your toe, getting stuck in traffic, receiving dirty looks or snide remarks from others, getting injured, unexpected expenses or bills in the mail, uneasy gut feelings, arguments with your loved ones, getting sick, headaches, losing or breaking your possessions, unpleasant odours, sounds or tastes.

Each of these signs is an indication that you need to center yourself and adjust your frequency. When you encounter one of these warning signs, just stop! Do not keep working on that task, or having that conversation, or obsessing over that thought you were just having because it is not taking you where you want to be. If you catch these warning signs quickly and respond immediately, the simple act of centering yourself will stop the negative momentum.

As a final note, try not to obsess over a warning sign. Talking about it, thinking about it, and replaying it over and over in your mind is a sure-fire way to lower your vibrational frequency. Take it for what it is, a simple "stop sign," and move on from it. Please take care of your vibration and only give attention to the thoughts, feelings, and actions that resonate with your soul's natural frequency.

Chapter 6

Effective Ways to Raise Your Vibration

Ayahuasca is a visionary plant medicine discovered by the Indigenous Amazonian people that greatly assists in raising your vibration. This medicine is an ancient healer and teacher that has been used for thousands of years by the Shipibo people, as well as over seventy different tribal ethnicities across from the Amazonia basin.

Ayahuasca allows us to go very deep within ourselves and heal past traumas and let go of that which no longer serves our highest purpose paving the way to be in a higher vibratory state.

This medicine can offer powerful guidance for your path and connects you with the energy of your heart, allowing you to move through fears that are holding you back in your life. The process can be very intense physically and emotionally.

This master plant creates a purging effect as blockages are being cleared from our physical and energetic bodies. This can manifest as vomiting, diarrhea, laughing, crying, yawning, shaking, etc. It is profound spiritual work that takes a lot of courage and trust. This medicine works with each participant in a unique way depending on what healing needs to take place.

It heals the body, cleanses the blood, the liver, and the gallbladder. There is an intelligent spirit behind the medicine. It clears out the emotional field by allowing us to process our old traumas and liberate ourselves from those things. It also brings our energy into the third eye and the crown chakras and allows us to experience multiple realms. This journey into the multiple realms helps us to realize that there is a vast, invisible reality out there. The invisible realms become visible with Ayahuasca. It is an incredibly nourishing experience.

Ayahuasca also opens up people's spirit so that they are willing to accept healing because many people have a vested interest in being sick or weak. There is nothing more frightful then being completely well because then you have to take responsibility for the world around you.

The way that Ayahuasca brings things to the surface for healing can be deeper than you could ever imagine, and this process truly benefits from the guidance and support of a trained Ayahuasca Shaman.

In their ceremonies Ayahuasca Shamans who have trained for years, and are not just a leaf in the wind, sing Arkanas which are protection songs that prevent negative forces from entering the space. They also do direct work on each person, singing Ikaros (power songs) to help remove and release the blockages they see in their participants. The Ikaros that are sung also help to invite good energy and good consciousness.

It is also vitally important to have trained facilitators as well at these powerful ceremonies. They hold the space and make sure the participants are kept safe and protected. Ayahuasca also works much better in its home which is Peru. Miraculous Ayahuasca ceremonies occur here because of this.

In closing, Ayahuasca is a tool, an initiation into what you need to do to change your life. It is the door opening, and the keys being handed to you. It is up to you now to walk through the door, to turn the handle, and to keep walking no matter how difficult or intense it can be. Ultimately it is you who heals yourself because Ayahuasca is only a tool which means it shows you things in a new, unique perspective.

Kambo is a traditional medicine used by many of the tribes of the Amazon rainforest and is an effective means to raise your vibration. A poison, Kambo is collected from the Phyllomedusa Bicolor frog. Like all of nature, the Kambo frog is revered by the tribes so it is returned to the jungle unharmed after the collection. When you work with Kambo you are reminded of the common bonds between all of life. Kambo is a master of alchemy, of systematically removing our blocks to Spirit. Kambo does this by purifying our personal distortions, impurities found on all five layers of our existence thus not only does Kambo clean our body, it works on the emotional, causal and spiritual levels of our being.

Kambo promotes the understanding of our feelings, by bringing up that which we have suppressed and since long forgotten. By removing these impurities, the remnants of unprocessed and unhealthy feelings from the past, we reveal layer by layer our authentic self. Kambo clears the path ahead promoting a deeper understanding of ourselves and everything around us. The clearer we become, the more resonant we get and the more we synchronize with "what is." In this enlightened state, happiness and joy are easy, because they are after all your natural state, that which you truly are.

Kambo's medicine washes away any negative physical and mental energies which deny us a balanced and peaceful life. When we have allowed emotional toxins to thwart our outlook on life, or when we feel swamped, it is surely time for Kambo. Many have described their Kambo experiences as a genuine rebirth, like walking through a portal after which they were never the same again.

Post Kambo, some people have realized their unrealized dreams and found ways to fulfill their heart's desires. Kambo helped them to reignite their courage and to acknowledge themselves on a deeper level, letting go of that which was holding them back and allowing them to embrace their highest happiness.

Whether Kambo has you purging, sweating, shaking, crying, or in a state of bliss, you can be sure that change is in progress. The frog is a Universal symbol of the embracing of personal power. It reminds us not to become bogged down with day to day living. Kambo is similar in nature to an octopus, deeply intelligent and responsive to the environment. Kambo is never the same because you are never the same. When you choose to work with Kambo, your experience is unique and cannot be known. A complete letting go of 'what you think' is happening allows a deepening of 'what is' actually happening. We learn from Kambo that fighting transformation is never comfortable nor wise, forever letting go is shown to be a more fruitful strategy.

Lastly, go to my YouTube Channel and I will show you, "Effective ways to Raise your Vibration." In the YouTube Search Engine type in **"Shelly Kadej."** – Weekly Videos posted.

Suggested Meditations to Raise your Vibration

1) I am open to receive peaceful, healing energy and the energies of renewal.

2) I infuse my relationships with the energy of love and acceptance.

3) Energies are moving and shifting, and coming together to give me exactly what I need and want.

4) Scattered energies do not serve me. I ground myself which will create a steady and calm energy, which will translate into secure and strong relationships with myself and others.

5) I am open to receiving a self-assured energy that enables me to improve current relationships and attract new ones as well.

6) I forgive my faults and rejoice in my perfect uniqueness.

7) The energy I am experiencing in this moment, is fluid and free rather than overly rigid and controlled. I release myself to this flow.

8) I understand that nothing is static. Life flows in cycles, expanding and contracting, changing and growing.

9) I welcome the energy of expansion because it will help me to grow into any new situation gracefully, safely, and comfortably.

10) I accept that things will happen when the time and energies are right.

11) I bring in the energies of awareness and

transformation with love.

12) I understand that ALL relationships must have an

even exchange of energy.

13) I choose to not block or close off my energy field.

If it does happen, I release this blocking energy by

working with affirmations, prayers, and my spirit

guides.

14) I allow for the powerful energy of love to surround

me because this loving, balance energy is needed for

healthy relationships to occur.

Chapter 7

Vibrational Medicine

Vibrational Medicine interfaces with subtle energy fields that underlie the functions of a physical body. It is based on the idea of resonant frequencies, similar to a tuned string on a musical instrument resonating with anything tuned to the same frequency, or an opera singer breaking a glass by singing at a certain pitch. Some sciences and philosophies have recognized vibrational elements, as an important part of the Universe. It is proving difficult to link these new sciences with the dogma of Western Medicine. Even as long ago as 1928, Thomas Sugrue recognized vibrational elements at work in the human body.

Vibrational Medicine is one of the most, if not the most

widely studied fields of medicine today.

There is now global interest and research in the clinical applications of Vibrational Medicine. Vibrational Medicine, of which Homeopathy is a part, has been used by various systems of medicine throughout the ages, but because of its subtle nature, until recently it has been largely ignored by the mainstream medical establishment. Fortunately, this is no longer the case. Advancements in modern technology have made it possible for the unseen/subtle to be seen. Researchers can now view and measure the body's subtle energy fields, as well as changes in these fields after vibrational modalities have been applied. With these findings has come a new surge of global interest, research, and discoveries in all systems of medicine vibrational in nature.

The human body is a multi-dimensional vibrational being with numerous complex energetic interactions continually taking place. These complex energetic interactions, a bio-energetics network emit vibratory information that precisely specify the activities taking place within the body, and these vibratory emissions are measureable with modern equipment. Current research hypothesizes that every part of the body – mental, physical, and emotional form this continuous interconnected bio-energetics communication network.

Each part of the body, even the smallest constituent, is part of the bio-energetic communication network, vibrational medicine stimulates this network, and the body's restorative systems respond without the side-effects associated with the use of pharmacological substances. Everything living vibrates at certain frequencies. This is true not only for molecules, cells, tissues, and organs, but also for parasites, bacterium, viruses, etc. Imbalances, disorders and diseases alter the bio-energetics communication network, and through the use of vibrational medical devices balance can be restored. Your body can then go to work healing itself.

Your body's innate intelligence loves you and is repairing the body every day and every moment until the time of your passing. Dis-ease (not disease) is a gift utilized within the body to bring awareness to your conscious that you are creating dis-ease within your system of reality. You need to evaluate dis-ease patterns and change them to align with what you are here to experience.

Health is purely your experience with yourself. All health professions and providers no matter what form, are essentially doing the same thing for the person being treated. They are stimulating the body to focus the innate intelligence of the body more acutely on an area of needed self-evaluation, be it sub-conscious or conscious. If given enough freedom of expression, the body will repair itself from any and all ailments in any form or stage of development/growth. If you are able to bring your state of focus more acutely to an area of need, then you will be able to harmonize the area or cells of dis-ease to the original intention of expression. At that point the diseased cells will resonate at their appropriate frequency and then start performing their tasks as originally intended. The resonance of all cells is different and dependent upon all of the vibrational and oscillatory beat frequencies of all material present to create their own unique heterodyne (beat) frequency. All of these trillions of cells combine to form our personal vibrational frequency rate.

Western Medicines approach to cancer and healing chronic diseases is chemical therapy to activate atomic changes in the body, radiation to damage a large enough volume of tissue to cause your immune system to clean up the tissue that is deemed no longer wanted. Also, surgery is used to cut out enough rogue cells so that the immune system can then take care of the rest of the cells on its own.

In conclusion, when Western Medicine works on the body, the typical approach is to create damage to force an immediate and dramatic innate response, or bring the tissue close enough together that the innate intelligence can work to repair the damaged tissue. Most other practitioners work to change the body's activity temporarily and long enough to force the innate intelligence to dedicate more resources to a specific area of increased need.

Eastern Medicines approach in western culture is to look for imbalances within the body. The next step is to try to restore harmony and balance within the body, hoping that it will then recognize that it is currently not working in harmony, and will change its operating patterns and start working properly. Western and Eastern Medicines are both trying to trigger your body, into a forced state of awareness, which requires action by either eliciting enough damage that you will either repair or die, or respectively shifting the body's internal environment so much that you are not able to express a physiological state of being that you desire.

Alternatively, if you are able to change your focus, your thoughts, and your vibrational expression which then changes the innate energy utilization in the body then remissions of healing can occur in this state. This is also the state that prayer and meditation will take you. In closing, belief is vitally important because if you do not believe it will happen then your body will bring about a physical response that provides you with that experience.

Chapter 8

What I have Learned

Your energy introduces you before you even speak.

When you change your heart, you change your Life.

Follow your heart, and synchronicity will unfold before your eyes.

The heart doesn't lie, only people do.

Learn to think without words; instead think with feelings.

Live from inside, not outside.

The Universe is within you.

We are stars wrapped in skin – the light you are seeking has always been within.

We are not just this physical body. Our presence doesn't end at our skin line. We have an energy field around us. This energy field connects us to other living beings and the Universe around us. We are all interconnected and each one of us has a unique energetic field, and we are part of the same divine brilliance that created the infinite cosmos. When we are in touch with this feeling of being part of the Divine, our true essence being love, then our energy vibrates at a high frequency. Our positive thoughts and feelings and healthy practices support a bright energy field.

The interior truth brings light and transparency.

Remove yourself from your achievements and live with serenity. Everything is temporary.

Your vision will become clear when you can look into your own heart.

Who looks outside dreams, who looks inside awakes.

When things flow you will find the answer(s) you are looking for.

The meaning of Life is Life.

There are no mistakes in Life, only lessons. Repeat until you learn!

When something truly begins in life, we first have to go through a tunnel.

Have faith in the future. Go across the bridge, and then what is new is no longer unfamiliar.

Only he who remains in a state of change, remains true to himself.

We may reckon with temporary upsets and a degree of insecurity when our life undergoes change. How else can we get around to casting off old habits and developing into

a new state of consciousness?

The dawn is not far away, but before you can reach the dawn the dark night has to be passed through. And as the dawn comes closer, the night will become darker.

There is a time for everything, and everything is important.

Investigate your experiences thoroughly and pursue those desires that radiate the greatest energy.

When you know what you're doing, you can do what you like.

One has to live forwards, but one can only understand it backwards.

First do what is necessary, then what's possible, and suddenly you're doing the impossible.

If you want to achieve great things, you must follow the flow of your spiritual energy.

Go with the flow. Following the flow of energy not only takes the least effort, but it also achieves the best results.

The human mind functions in the same way as respiration. It is calm and relaxed when it is allowed to proceed undisturbed in its own rhythm.

There is no greater feeling then realizing that your life starts NOW.

Everything happens for you, not to you.

When the heart mourns for what it has lost, the Spirit rejoices for what it has found.

Loneliness is absence of the other. Aloneness is the presence of oneself.

Complete autonomy, along with harmony and equality with all other souls, a state that can be described as "collective oneness" within which we feel connected to all other souls, while at the same time maintaining our own individuality

99

and personal soul identity.

Wounds heal if they are treated properly.

Pain is not to make you miserable, the pain is to make you aware. And when you are aware, misery disappears.

Just remember you die if you worry, you die if you don't.

The longest journey you'll ever take is the one where you need to find yourself.

As long as you stay true to your path, everything you do is worthwhile. Equally, the greatest achievements are valueless if they do not serve to further your progress on the way of your wishes. The path is its own goal.

Birth is not a momentary event, but a permanent process. Our aim in life is to become completely born... living means born every minute. We need this permanent state of being born, i.e. self-determined modelling of our lives in a way that is not regulated by habit or routine, but through our own free choice and free will. This means replacing conformist behavior(s) and conventional thinking with a style of life that is truly our own.

When you are evolving to your higher self, the road seems lonely. But you're simply shedding energies that no longer match the frequency of your destiny.

Your challenge is to learn to understand your part as an individual in the big picture, to understand how order is born out of chaos, and how we as humans emerge from the cosmic soup to live our lives and contribute our unique role within the whole.

Once you establish what your unique role is in the bigger picture, you'll understand how your dynamic contribution is integral to the functioning of the whole. You'll blossom as a result of casting off your secret fears and doubts, your aggression and frustration, and draw on your resourcefulness to reveal the truly adventurous and courageous person you really are.

The road to enlightenment is the transformation from a life of longings and cravings to one of release and energetic satisfaction.

To be enlightened is to be able to be at peace with the is, and to find the beauty in every moment, person, experience and lesson, because no matter how dark life may get, if your light is always shining you will always find your way.

Just be appreciative of the adversity, and grateful for the beauty, and you will be just fine.

When we speak of being "grounded" or "centered" it is this Source we are talking about. There is a vast reservoir of energy available to us, and that we tap into it not by thinking and planning, but by getting grounded, centered, and silent enough to be in contact with the Source. It is within each of us, like a personal individual sun giving us life and nourishment. Pure energy pulsating and available, is ready to give us anything we need to accomplish something, and ready to welcome us back home when we want to rest.

The "New Prosperity, Abundance Flow," is available to us if we can remain in the NOW moment, be unattached, be clear in our vibration and fully expressed with and from Integrity, Love and Respect.

Burn your boats when you have reached the other shore.

The way to find out who you are is not by comparing yourself with others, but by looking to see whether you are fulfilling your own potential in the best way you know how.

How do you choose to define yourself? Who you choose to be right now, will not be the same in all moments and experiences. The true self is expressed when you choose the expression of your authentic self that suits the moment/

experience at the instance that it is occurring, never before and never after, without any history or future direction. If you do not clearly define yourself consciously, then you allow your subconscious to redefine you based on the most dominant personality that you are interacting with. All of that being said, there's a fun time to be had in both expressions. Any interaction with another causes you to define yourself.

A man's true life is the way in which he puts off the lie imposed by others on him. Stripped, naked, natural, he is what he is. This is a matter of being, and not of becoming. The lie cannot become the truth, the personality cannot become your soul. There is no way to make the nonessential the essential. The nonessential remains nonessential and the essential remains essential, they are not convertible. And striving towards truth is nothing but creating more confusion. The truth has not to be achieved. It cannot be achieved, it is already the case. Only the lie has to be dropped. All aims and ideals and goals and ideologies, religions and systems of improvement and betterment, are lies. Beware of them. Recognize the fact that as you are, you are a lie because you have been manipulated and cultivated by others. Striving

after truth is a distraction and a postponement. It is the lie's way to hide. See the lie, look deep into the lie of your personality. Because to see the lie is to cease to lie. No longer to lie is to seek no more for any truth – there is no need, the moment the lie disappears, truth is there in all its beauty and radiance. In the seeing of the lie it disappears, and what is left is the truth.

By being yourself, you will naturally attract the relationship that will serve you best.

Expose the false voices that tell you that you're unworthy, and silence them.

Everything about you is valuable if you just take it into your possession.

Life isn't a business to be managed, it's a mystery to be lived.

There can't be a "we" until there is a "me."

Two halves do not make a whole in relationships. You must be whole yourself.

It is not a sign of disaster and certainly nothing to be ashamed of – in fact it is usually a sign of quality – when the problematical aspects of a relationship come out into the open.

Resistance is Futile, Solitude is Bliss.

Real fearlessness is the product of tenderness. It comes from letting the world tickle your heart, your raw and beautiful heart. You are willing to open up, without resistance or shyness, and face the world. You are willing to share your heart with others.

Whenever we move into the new and unknown with the trusting spirit of a child, innocent and open and vulnerable, even the smallest things of life can become the greatest adventures. Insecurity is the only way to grow, to face danger is the only way to grow, to accept the challenge(s) of the unknown is the only way to grow.

Don't resist, just embrace.

The absence of fear is unconditional love.

Love others without conditions or circumstances.

Try not to confuse "attachment" with "love." Attachment is about fear and dependency, and has more to do with love of self, than love of another. Love without attachment is the purest love, because it isn't about what others can give you because you're empty. It is about what you can give others because you're already full.

Love is an attitude. Try it at work and in the home – you will achieve much more that way than any other. A great-minded life is one lived in and with conscious love.

Empathy, not sympathy! Love, share, but don't identify yourself with other people's emotions.

A person can stand anything if they can stand themselves.

Love yourself and then you can marry anybody.

Invent rules that are good for you and stick to them.

Fear not, judge not, resist not.

What is True Power? It is not a force (push or pull), not pressure, not giving, but much simpler. True Power is the "presence that you are."

You cannot decide direction, you can only live in the moment that is available to you. By living it, direction arises.

A life truly lived constantly burns away veils of illusion, burns away what is no longer relevant, gradually reveals our essence, until, at last, we are strong enough to stand in our naked truth.

As with everything in life, the beginning is woven into the end, and the end eventually leads to a new beginning. Starting something new offers excitement and opportunity for change. Although, often saying hello to the new, means saying goodbye to what you know.

New beginnings are often disguised as painful endings.

Follow your passion, and you will find your purpose.

Pour your energy into life and watch you and everyone around you change.

The more joy you add to your life, the greater the energy level and the higher the vibration, bringing beautifully renewed vitality.

Things change very fast once we set an intention, align with the vibration of **ALL** our desires, and then take massive action. We construct our entire world based upon vibrational states of expression.

Your wishes should serve you and your happiness, and not the other way around. The aim of wish fulfillment is to be happy without any more wishes.

The truth is what bears fruit. To have a talent and not use it, means to misuse it.

The greatest talents remain worthless if they do not contribute to the benefit of others.

Being human is the doorway to the Divine. Technique, expertise and knowledge are just tools; the key is to abandon oneself to the energy that fuels the birth of all things. This energy has no form or structure, yet all the forms and structures come out of it.

When you relate to thoughts obsessively, you are actually feeding them because thoughts need your attention to survive. Once you begin to pay attention to them and categorize them, then they become very powerful. You are feeding them energy because you are not seeing them as simple phenomena. If one try's to quiet them down, that is another way of feeding them.

Once you start dropping thoughts, the dust that you have collected in the past, the flame arises – clean, clear, alive, young. Your whole life becomes a flame without any smoke. That is what awareness is.

There is nothing either good or bad, but thinking makes it so. *Without* the human mind, things just happen, and they are not good or bad, beautiful or ugly. A weed is only a weed when we don't like it. Children are only naughty if we don't like their actions. Life only sucks if you judge it as bad. But what about truly horrible tragedies, like a plague or tsunami or the Holocaust? Surely these are bad? Sure, through the lens of the judgment we've been raised to make, they are terrible. But then again, remove the judgment, and then they simply happened. Death and cruelty will probably always make us sad, but they've always happened and always will, whether we like them or hate them.

See life in all its dimensions, from the depths to the heights. They exist altogether, and when we come to know from experience that the dark and the difficult are needed as much as the light and easy, then we begin to have a very different perspective on the world. By allowing all of life's colors to penetrate us, we become more integrated.

Remember that the events in your life are meaningless, unless you tell them what they are. By this, I mean that circumstances don't matter, only state of being matters. Because state of being materializes everything around you. It's up to you what meaning you give to the things that happen to you.

Time changes, the world goes on changing, but the experience of silence, the joy of it, remains the same. That is the only thing you can rely upon, the only thing that never dies. It is the only thing you can call your very being.

Trust the silence, there's a moment in it.

If you are depressed, you are living in the past. If you are anxious, you are living in the future. If you are at peace, you are living in the present.

If the actions or words that you speak do not make you calmer and centered, find the actions or words that will. It can profoundly change your reactive energy.

Before you speak, let your words pass through three gates: Is it true? Is it necessary? Is it kind?

When we find ourselves in a situation in which our buttons are being pushed, we can choose to repress or act out, or we can choose to practice. If we can start to do the exchange, breathing in with the intention of keeping our hearts open to the embarrassment or fear or anger that we feel, then to our surprise we find that we are also open to what the other person is feeling. "Open heart is Open heart."

Spending time with someone who drains you is a form of theft – they are stealing your peace of mind.

To set free disillusionment, recognize the illusion, learn the new lesson which will set a huge amount of energy free.

When you are at a place where you can be free of all of the things you are overly attached to, you have gained a freedom which has given you exactly what you thought the other things would deliver but didn't.

The moment you start clinging to things, you have missed the target – you have missed. Because things are not the target, you, your innermost being is the target – not a beautiful house, but a beautiful you; not much money, but a rich you; not many things, but an open being, available to millions of things.

The most beautiful people we have known are those who have known defeat, known suffering, known struggle, known loss, and have found their way out of the depths. These persons have an appreciation, a sensitivity, and an understanding of life that fills them with compassion, gentleness, and a deep loving concern. Beautiful people do not just happen.

We were born to experience an entire range of emotions. It is our destiny to experience bliss and sadness, joy as well as depression, and love as well as anger. It is healthy for us to have a wide range of emotions, this is part of the experience of being human. Having emotions goes along with being passionate about life and how we fully engage in it. Repressing emotions creates stagnant energy, which leads to both emotional and physical illness.

Times of great sorrow have the potential to be times of great transformation. But in order for transformation to happen we must go deep, to the very roots of our pain and experience it as it is, without blame or self-pity.

Emotional loss teaches you the lesson of impermanence. Life never stays as it is. Good times come and go and so do people. Irrevocable loss is often suggested by the number 5 and the sense that nothing will ever be the same again. You must all learn to accept loss as part of life, trusting that once you are prepared to let go, the Universe will replace your loss with something of equal worth or better.

Forgiveness cannot be forced. As you continue to be empowered by the movement happening from living an authentic life, you will feel a desire to release those who anchor you to your past. You will begin to acknowledge how people in your past mirrored and reflected back to you your personal issues to be explored and healed. In time you will find yourself compelled to release and forgive the people in your life from your past who no longer mirror back to you the truth of who you are and who you have become. Trust your timing. You will know when it is time to break the cord that binds you to an identity that you no longer feel connected to. This will bring you to a state of freedom you have been yearning for. Because once you release these relationships, you can attract people and situations into your life that reflect back to you your new awareness and state of health.

Guilt is one of the most destructive emotions in which we can get caught up into. If we have wronged another, or gone against our own truth, then of course we will feel bad. But to let ourselves be overwhelmed with guilt is to invite more guilt. We end up surrounded by nagging clouds of self-doubt and feelings of worthlessness to the point where we cannot see any of the beauty and joy that life is trying to offer us.

We all long to be better people – more loving, more aware, more true to ourselves. But when we punish ourselves for our failures by feeling guilty, we can get locked into a cycle of despair and hopelessness that robs us of all clarity about ourselves, and the situations we encounter. You are absolutely okay as you are, and it is absolutely natural to go astray from time to time. Just learn from it, move on, and use the lesson not to make the same mistake again.

Travelling through the transitional zone is actually a prolonged death process. It is the dying away of the old to make way for the new – the new Divine you. This process is definitely not easy, death processes never are, and it will certainly challenge you right to the core – and beyond even that. However, just remember the tools and remember to use them continuously… accepting, letting go, releasing, allowing, living in the Divine moment, and trusting in self.

Q: Why do you think that people are so protective of their egos? Why is it so hard to let go of one's ego?

A: People are afraid of the emptiness of space, or the absence of company, the absence of a shadow. It could be a terrifying experience to have no one to relate to, nothing to relate with. The idea of it can be extremely frightening, though not the real experience. It generally is a fear of space, a fear that we will not be able to anchor ourselves to any solid ground, that we will lose our identity as a fixed and solid and definite thing. This could be very threatening.

The image we have of ourselves comes not from our own direct experience, but from the opinion of others. A 'personality' imposed from the outside replaces the individuality that could have grown from within. We become just another sheep in the herd, unable to move freely, and unconscious of our own true identity. Unless you drop your personality, you will not be able to find your individuality. Individuality is given by existence; personality is imposed by society. Personality is social convenience.

It is time to break free of whatever you have been conditioned by others to believe about yourself. Dance, run, jog, and do gibberish, whatever is needed to wake up the sleeping lion from within.

Your reality is created from within yourself. Everything you see on the outside in your life is a reflection of your thoughts, beliefs, and emotions you hold inside. Like a mirror, you are getting reflections of what's inside you.

Other people are giving you the opportunity to improve yourself by letting you see what they're doing. If you don't like what they're doing, ask yourself, "What am I doing along the same lines?"

For example, if you've been treated like second place in a

relationship, perhaps the Universe is reflecting how you treat yourself. If you don't put yourself first, why should others?

Believe and you shall receive.

Everything combined that makes up our material Universe is dependent upon our Will of Intention and Direction of Action.

Nothing happens unless we make it so. It's never easy, but no one ever said life was going to be. What you accumulate doesn't amount to being successful or happy; it's how you live and what you are willing to give back.

The best way to facilitate an awakening in others is to lead by example. There is nothing you need to do, you must only be, because the being is the doing, and soon others will become by proxy.

It is important to be responsible to others, but it is inappropriate to be responsible for others. We cannot grow for others. "It is not our job to push dead bears up trees."

Lately I've been replacing my "I'm sorry" with "thank you's," like instead of "sorry I'm late," I'll say "thanks for waiting for me," or instead of "sorry for being such a mess," I'll say "thank-you for loving me and caring about me unconditionally." It has not only shifted the way I think and feel about myself, but also improved by relationships with others who now get to receive my gratitude instead of my negativity.

Each person brings something new into the world. This newness needs a chance to develop.

Every person who reveals what is sacred is a spiritual teacher for everybody else.

"That's how we have done it for the past twenty years!" Maybe, but you could have been doing it wrong for the past twenty years!

The past is created from the present and not the other way around. The only moment in time that actually exists is NOW. Everything that has ever happened is just a remembering of that event in this very moment. And whenever you bring things from past into the present, you can give a different meaning to them, and in the end, change your whole history. In this sense, you are a different individual with every second, with every NOW.

Summary

Einstein's famous equation E=MC2 with Love being the binding agent within this equation. Love is the exact vibration that matter responds to. Healing takes place only when love is present. In the late 80's, research was done to see if all healers might have something in common. Many healers were looked at most of whom used different forms or techniques. It was found that the energies coming off of their bodies had an almost identical sine-wave signature, the same pattern of three high waves and one low wave that continuously repeated, and that the source of this pattern was located in the Universal heart chakra, which is the primary chakra of Universal unconditional love.

From this research, it is now believed that whatever healing technique(s) a person uses is of little importance. The technique(s) simply gives the healer a structure for the mind of that person to focus on, but the real healing comes from the love that the healer is giving to the person being healed. The healer's love for that person heals and their knowledge. So speaking of healing without speaking of love will always evade the truth. Healing people, healing villages or healing the entire planet is all the same. The only difference is simply the greater degree of love.

Also important here is that things change easily once the mind can accept the healing. The whole body is seen as energy, including any disease(s). It does not matter what the story is around the disease, or what the person thinks caused the disease because both the body and the disease are just energy. It is easiest to heal if the old negative diseased energy is removed before attempting to put positive energy back into the body.

In addition, the mind has the knowledge to manipulate matter, but love has the power to not only manipulate matter, but to effortlessly create matter from nothing. No matter what the problem is that needs to be healed, love can always find a way. True love has no limits.

What is the veil that keeps us from seeing and living this great truth? It is the belief patterns we hold onto that limit us. What we believe to be true is always our limitation. If our doctor's tell us that a certain disease is incurable and we believe them, we cannot heal ourselves. We remain frozen in that belief. We must then live out that belief even if it means living in great pain and discomfort for the rest of our lives. Only a miracle which is something much greater than ourselves can overcome a frozen belief. So, it is our minds that can arrest a healing. When our minds are in control and not our hearts, we will almost always suffer. When we truly believe it is possible to be healed, we can do it ourselves.

"What you believe to be true is always your limitation.

If you do not believe in limitations, you are free."

Healing others – You don't have the right to heal anybody you want even if you could go around and touch everybody, and they'd be absolutely healed because it is illegal. This is a school we live in, and everybody's experience is their own experience and they need it. You can't heal someone just because you want to or they need or deserve it. You have to get permission first.

Why get permission? – We cannot see very well from this position within the third dimension. We do not know what our actions are really going to do in the bigger picture. We may think that we are doing this person great good by healing him or her when in fact we are harming them. We all live in a Universal school of remembering.

An illness may be just what that person came to Earth for. Through this illness this person may learn compassion, and by healing him or her it takes away that possibility. Keep your ego out of the way, and healing will come naturally.

You can bring your body and your world into perfect balance with love. Life flows and becomes easy and not diseasy. Native tribes in the world believe that we have this higher aspect (higher selves) within us. If we can make the connection with love and conscious communication, we then can get clear guidance from within us about how to move moment by moment in life. The movements become filled with grace and power, with little or no effort. This guidance comes from only you, and it cares about you in the same way you care about yourself.

Only from the present or moment to moment can we truly experience everything. The present is usually too painful for most people to participate in. Our adult lives are deadened and we are only living a shadow of what is humanly possible. Connection to our higher selves cannot be attained through force or determination, or through any amount of begging or crying, or feeling sorry for ourselves. This behavior will not connect us to our higher selves.

Only love, innocence, and a great deal of patience will allow you to find your way. You can forget about trying. You simply must live life from your heart and not your mind. Your mind will function, but under the control of your heart.

Once you are connected consciously to your higher self, life becomes a completely different experience from anything you have known before. Life works through you, and your words and actions have great power. Nothing is outside you, everything is within you. And the truth of who you really are will begin to unfold. It becomes clear that everything is alive and once that realization becomes your life, then everything becomes communication and everything has meaning. Once connected, your entire reality becomes alive and fully conscious, and everything is communicating and does not require asking for an answer. It comes from within, and it comes from within the heart, not the mind. There is a certainty without a doubt like knowing your own name, and it is this certainty that allows knowingness to emerge from the heart. Along with this knowingness there is a loss of wanting to know.

As long as we continue to judge the events in our lives, we give power to them as either good or bad, which determines the course of our lives. To end it and then transcend it, we must step outside this polarity. We must change, and this change has to come in some way from our not judging this world. For it is in judging that we decide that something is either good or bad. That is the basis of good and evil, a duality consciousness. The key seems to be in viewing all the worlds in our Universe and all events within them as whole, complete, and perfect. We understand and know that the cosmic DNA, the cosmic plan, is proceeding exactly as directed by the Creator.

We must also understand and know that all energy is connected and because thoughts are created with energy, they can definitely impact our Universe. There have been numerous studies that have been conducted about how positive thoughts can impact a person's ability to get well. And, they have gotten well against all odds. The Buddhist Monks have also shown us ways the mind's thoughts can be used to slow a person's heart rate and breathing down.

The mind, body, and spirit are always working together perfectly to create exactly what we want and ask for. The emotional expressions that we associate with and create with every action or movement, is what guides other reactions to our chosen expression(s). There is no good or bad emotions as all are equally valid and true. Happiness and sadness are both equally valid expressions. Your chosen repeated expression(s) will become mirrored and patterned in the body physiology, which then produces changes in the body, due to repeated expressions of the same emotional state.

"Time" is the platform and buffer that delays our thought expressions into reality. If our thoughts were to come true the moment we thought them, we would destroy ourselves within minutes or hours depending upon how we view ourselves.

In closing, everything else not related to our current goal is a distraction from us finding our true selves and the actual expression that we came here to present. Radio, television, and movies can trigger thought expressions in-line with our true interests. Right now in its current forms it is more of a distraction and time waster, delaying our growth and choice to be expressive by programming our belief systems to one that is not really yours. Identify and live by your own true expression of life and interests, and you will live without dis-ease as you will always take actions that are aligned to your greatest good. You will in turn not repeat an action or actions that will lead to dis-ease which in turn will create a physiological response that is in-line with your chosen focus on a narrow set of emotional expressions.

"We are truly blessed in all that we are which blesses us in all that we do. The energy/intention of what we are looking for WILL come back to us ten-fold. We will also be blessed with the guidance of being shown the next step for transformation."

S.D. Raine

As human beings, our greatness lies not so much in being able to remake the world, that is the myth of the atomic age. Our greatness lies in being able to remake ourselves.

It is important to remember that we have been perfect since the day we were born. However, everyday experiences/labels/ judgments/ and expectations others have placed upon us, or that we have placed upon ourselves, have greatly clouded that perfection over.

The Universe is the Source of all gifts and talents, and we are the caretakers of these gifts. The gifts that I am a caretaker of include: Spiritual Teacher, Transformational Coach, Vibrational Healer, Mediumship (making contact with those that have passed on), Clairvoyance (the ability to see visions and images), and Tarot Cards (past/present/future).

Shelly is available for phone consultations, by

appointment only.

Email: ommuni8@gmail.com

YouTube: Shelly Kadej (S.D. Raine)

Weekly Videos posted on "Effective ways to Raise your

Vibration."

Made in the USA
San Bernardino, CA
18 October 2018